I am

Written by Diana Kimpton

Illustrated by Lisa Williams

I am hot.
What can I do?

I can take off my jumper.

I can have
a cold drink.

I can sit in the shade.

I can fan my face.

I can sit in the pool.

What can they do?

I am cold.

I am tired.

I am hungry.

I am dirty.